My First Story of Easter

Tim Dowley

Illustrated by Roger Langton

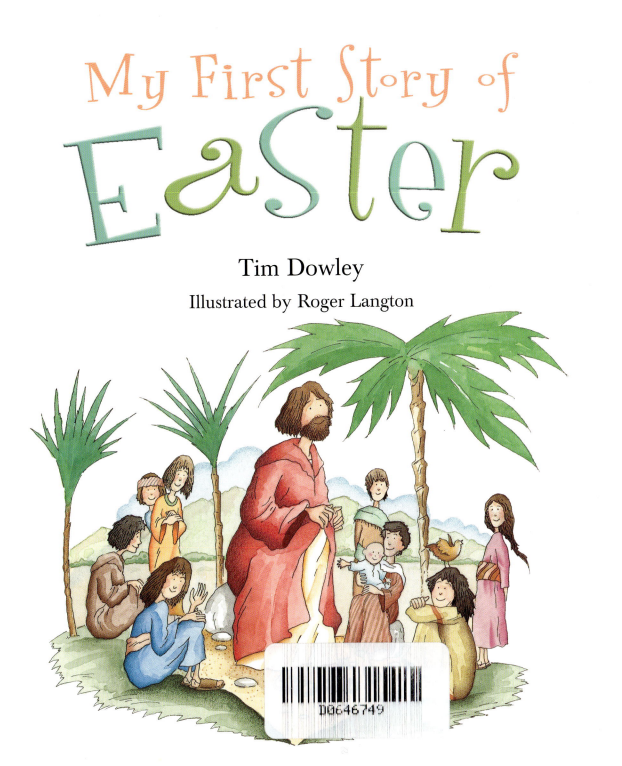

Cover design: Barb Fisher, LeVan Fisher Design

Worldwide co-edition produced by Lion Hudson plc, Mayfield House, 256 Banbury Road Oxford OX2 7DH, England

Tel: +44 (0) 1865 302750
Fax: +44 (0) 1865 302757
e-mail: coed@lionhudson.com
www.lionhudson.com

ISBN: 0·8024·1767·1
EAN/ISBN-13: 978·0·802417·67·1

Printed in Singapore

Since 1894, Moody Publishers has been dedicated to equip and motivate people to advance the cause of Christ by publishing evangelical Christian literature and other media for all ages around the world. Because we are a ministry of the Moody Bible Institute of Chicago, a portion of the proceeds from the sale of this book go to train the next generation of Christian leaders.

If we may serve you in any way in your spiritual journey toward understanding Christ and the Christian life, please contact us at www.moodypublishers.com.

Jesus of Nazareth was the friend of many.
He told great stories.
He healed sick people and did wonderful miracles.

There was an important festival in Jerusalem.
Jesus went with twelve special friends, his disciples.

Jesus borrowed a donkey and rode into Jerusalem.
The crowds became very excited.
They shouted and waved palm-tree branches.

But some of the priests hated Jesus
and plotted to kill him.

On the day of the festival,
Jesus ate a special supper
with his disciples in an upstairs room.

Jesus broke bread and gave it to his disciples.
But one disciple, Judas, was plotting against him.

He crept out.

After supper, Jesus took his disciples to a garden outside the city. 'Stay here and pray,' he told them.

Jesus prayed too.
Then a crowd of Jesus' enemies appeared, led by Judas.

The soldiers took Jesus away.

They stood Jesus before the Roman ruler, Pilate.

'Jesus is a trouble-maker,' said the priest. 'He should be killed!'

'I can find nothing wrong with him,' said Pilate.

But the people shouted, *'Kill him, kill him!'* So Pilate sent Jesus to die.

Cruel men pushed a crown made of thorns on Jesus' head.
Then they led him out of the city.

When they reached a hill,
soldiers nailed Jesus to a wooden cross.
They also fixed two robbers on crosses.
Jesus said, 'Father, forgive them.'

One robber asked, 'Jesus, remember me.'
Jesus said, 'Today, you will be with me in heaven.'

At midday the sky went dark. Jesus cried out and died.
Jesus' family and friends watched sadly.

A good man called Joseph took Jesus' body. He put it in a rock tomb and rolled a huge stone across the door.

Early on Sunday morning,
women went to the tomb.
The stone was rolled away – but they couldn't see Jesus' body.

Suddenly two shining men stood there.
'Jesus isn't *here!*' said one. 'He is risen from the dead.'

The women rushed back to tell the disciples.
At first they didn't believe the women.

But then Jesus
appeared to them.

And after this
Jesus appeared to many
of his friends.

Once, Jesus cooked breakfast for his disciples
beside a lake.

A few weeks later, Jesus was taken up
into heaven again. The disciples watched.

At Easter we remember that Jesus died.

And that he is alive for ever.